HEALTHY EATING
FOR FAMILIES

The Ultimate Nutrition Guide
for Kids, Parents, and Educators

STARRING THE

SUPER CREW

Melissa Halas, MA, RDN, CDE

ISBN: 978-1-7339692-7-7

Visit
SuperKidsNutrition.com
For more fun, healthy & tasty ideas!

To the parents, educators, and caretakers who nourish our children with good nutrition, support, love, and care.

DEAR PARENT CAREGIVER, OR TEACHER,

I'm so glad you have decided to share this book with your child or student. Here are some tips on how to use this book.

First, read the book yourself, taking your time to go through it. Then, once you are familiar with the content, read through the book at home or in the classroom with your children or students.

It's best to tackle one to two character sections at a time, so children don't get overwhelmed. Then, focus on one new activity each week. For example, this week, try adding a new color fruit, vegetable, or bean. Remember, change happens over time, not overnight.

Don't miss the tips for parents, caregivers, and teachers at the back of the book. Try practicing a couple of new tips each week. It's easy for old habits to come back, so re-read the book and keep practicing new habits.

Remember this is a book you'll read again and again! Get more tips on how to use this book and feeding your family at SuperKidsNutrition.com/Healthy-Eating-Book.

♡ The Super Crew ♡
&
Melissa

Meet
the SUPER CREW

The Super Crew gets superpowers from eating tasty, colorful foods from plants.
Learn what powers *you* can get from eating healthy whole foods from nature.

Super Baby Abigail

Power:
Flies and has x-ray
vision and super smarts!
Power changes based
on the foods she eats.
Power Foods:
Plant foods of all colors,
especially blueberries.

Tom-Tom

Power:
Moves and
shapes water.
Power Foods:
Water and red foods,
like watermelon,
red apples, and
red tomatoes.

Jessie

Power:
Changes the form
of objects.
Power Foods:
Green foods like
avocado, lettuce,
and kiwi.

Penny

Power:
Moves at super speed.
Power Foods:
Purple foods like
raisins and eggplant.

Kira

Power:
Camouflages with nature and levitates (floats above the ground).
Power Foods:
Brown foods like whole grains, cinnamon, and walnuts.

Carlos

Power:
Creates clouds and stink bombs.
Power Foods:
White foods like mushrooms, garlic, and white beans.

Andy

Power:
Has super strength.
Power Foods:
Orange foods like mangos, pumpkins, and sweet potatoes.

Marcus

Power:
Creates heat and has healing powers.
Power Foods:
Yellow foods like lemons, pineapple, and yellow squash.

Quack the duck

Cinnamon the dog

Pinkie the fish

Flutter the butterfly

MEET SUPER BABY ABIGAIL

"Hi, I am Super Baby Abigail. I get my powers from all colors of plant-based food. I'm always discovering new tastes and textures with each new food I try.

Eating colorful, delicious foods helps you to grow, stay healthy and strong, and feel your best. My favorite color is **blue** for **blueberries** and **blue corn**, my two F-A-V-O-R-I-T-E foods! I like to make tasty and nutritious foods with my friends."

Super Baby Abigail gets her powers from colorful plant foods like:

- **red - raspberry**
- orange - tangerine
- yellow - corn
- **green - baby spinach**
- blue - blueberry

- purple - prunes
- **white/beige - cauliflower**
- **black - black beans**
- brown - whole wheat

"I like to eat colorful plant-based foods to help me run fast, jump high, and supercharge my brain."

— Super Baby Abigail

Let's Talk:

"This week, I'm going to eat these colorful and flavorful foods."

- Frozen blueberries as a cold sweet treat
- Red and green bell peppers with hummus, ranch dip, or Greek yogurt dressing
- Black beans and salsa in a cheese quesadilla with broccoli

– Super Baby Abigail

 Your Turn:

Be a superstar like Super Baby Abigail and eat all the different plant food colors for good health. Name which colorful foods you're going to try this week by writing them below, on a separate piece of paper, or share out loud!

 Tip: I Tried It!

Do you like tomato sauce? Roasted or cooked vegetables like carrots, sweet potatoes, or onions can be added in small amounts to tomato sauce. Try blending these veggies in. It can help you become familiar with their taste.

Activity: Plant-Based Foods That Are Close to Nature

Colorful plant-based foods include fruits, vegetables, whole grains, beans, nuts, seeds, and herbs and spices, like basil and cinnamon.

- Plant foods have vitamins, minerals, and many powerful plant compounds. The Super Crew calls these powerful plant compounds "fight-o-nutrients" (phytonutrients) because they help fight off disease. They also have fiber to fill you up, and they taste really good. Both children and adults need all of these nutrients for a healthy body!

- Most of the time, try to eat plant-based foods in their natural state, so you really get to enjoy their taste.

Guess which of these foods is in its most natural state?

| Apple Sauce | Apples | Apple Juice |

| Potato Chips | French Fries | Baked Potatoes |

Answer:

- If you guessed apples and baked potatoes, you're right! These foods are more filling and give you longer-lasting energy.

- Store-bought applesauce with no added sugar can be a good choice, but fresh apples have more fiber and nutrients.

- When potatoes are made into potato chips or fries, they can lose a lot of important nutrients and that real potato taste. So, eating them closer to nature is best.

Balanced meals are one of the keys to good health.

Be like Super Baby Abigail, and use the MyPlate method to balance your meals. This helps you get the nutrition you need from all of the food groups every day. A healthy breakfast may only have three food groups. Sometimes lunch and dinner meals may only have four food groups, but try your best to get all five.

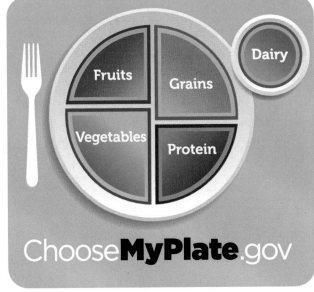

- The five food groups include fruits, vegetables, grains, protein, and dairy (or dairy substitutes).

- When you include more food groups, your meals are balanced because they have what you need to be super healthy!

- Try it and see how filling and satisfying it is to eat from different food groups instead of eating a single food.

Let's Talk:

Together, talk about what you like to eat most often at mealtimes.

- Which food groups do you eat the most?

- Which food groups do you eat the least?

- What are ways you can start adding more of the groups you don't eat as much? On the next page, you can make a plan.

I love helping my mom shop for healthy, tasty food.

Your Turn:

Come up with some meal ideas with your child that match the MyPlate image. See how many food groups you can add. Make a goal of at least three for breakfast and four to five at lunch and dinner. If you are starting with two groups, just try to add one more at first. It's okay to take it slow!

Together, write down three healthy and flavorful meal ideas below:

_____

_____

_____

Using what you've learned about MyPlate, draw a balanced meal below or on a new piece of paper.

Activity: Family Goal Setting

Let's play Start-Stop-Keep to make a nutritious plate! Name one healthy habit you will start today, one habit you will stop today, and one habit that is good for your body that you will keep on doing.

Start

Examples: (1) Start eating breakfast on school days. (2) Include a sweet fruit or savory vegetable at breakfast at least four times a week.

_____

Stop

Examples: (1) Stop drinking soda and choose water instead. (2) Stop adding salt and try a new herb or spice for a flavor boost.

_____

Keep

Examples: (1) Continue eating fruit for dessert. (2) Continue eating salad with dinner.

_____

Super Baby Abigail's Fun Food Fact:

Veggies can change the color of your smoothies without changing their sweet taste. I put baby spinach in my blueberry breakfast smoothie to make a yummy green shake!

– Super Baby Abigail

MEET TOM-TOM

"Hi, I am Tom-Tom. I get my powers from **red foods** and love their taste. I can move and shape water when I eat **red foods** or drink water. I'm always getting into trouble because when I laugh or play, I sometimes get carried away. Drinking water and eating **red foods** helps me create showers on a sunny day."

Tom-Tom gets his powers from red foods like:

- apples
- tomatoes
- watermelon
- red radish
- red pepper
- cherries
- strawberries
- beets
- raspberries
- pomegranate

"Red foods, like watermelon and beets, are good for your heart! I choose water first when I'm thirsty. I like red foods because they taste so good."

– Tom-Tom

Did you know that water helps:
- moisturize your skin
- make your tears
- make your saliva (so you can digest food)

Eating red foods helps:
- protect your body and heart
- improve your memory

Tip: Drinking Water is Important!

- Drink water to make sure your mouth makes saliva. You don't want to become dry like a desert! Saliva is the water in your mouth that we sometimes call spit.

- Without saliva, you can't swallow, chew, or taste your yummy food. It also helps keep your mouth and teeth clean. Saliva even fights germs and gives you good breath!

Activity: Making Flavorful Water

Add frozen fruit, chopped fresh fruit, or sliced vegetables to your water or herbal tea. Store in the refrigerator for up to three days. You can start with one of Tom-Tom's favorite foods and mix it with a fruit or vegetable you like.

Your Turn: What flavor combinations will you try?

Examples: (1) Lemon (2) Strawberry-cucumber (3) Orange-pineapple

1. _____

2. _____

3. _____

Tom-Tom's Fun Food Fact:

In 2013, the Guinness Book of World Records gave a prize to a person who grew a 350-pound watermelon. That's as much as a lion weighs!

– Tom-Tom

Water RULES!

Water is so good for your body!
Water helps keep you happy, healthy and feeling good!
Remember to drink water when playing and
when eating meals and snacks.

MEET ANDY

"Hi, I am Andy. I get my powers from **orange foods**, and they make me super strong. Sometimes I have to carry the Super Crew when we are exploring. I love the outdoors and sports. I love trying all new foods, but **orange foods** are my favorite. They taste good and give me super strength!"

Andy gets his powers from orange foods like:

- pumpkin
- sweet potato
- mango
- papaya
- persimmon
- peaches

- cantaloupe
- oranges
- apricots
- carrots
- butternut squash

"Orange foods have beta-carotene, a 'fight-o-nutrient' that makes Vitamin A. Orange foods help me go on outdoor adventures with the Super Crew. I love climbing trees, rock climbing, and building forts."

– Andy

Did you know that orange foods **help:**

- protect your heart and skin
- heal cuts faster
- keep your eyes healthy and even help you to see in the dark

Activity: Game Time

Can you name these foods? Look at each food picture to unscramble the word. Then draw a line to match the food to its picture. With a family member or friend, name the ways you like to eat Andy's favorite foods or new ways you plan to try them.

kupnmip _ _ _ _ _ _ _ _

rarotsc _ _ _ _ _ _ _

goanm _ _ _ _ _

sraonge _ _ _ _ _ _ _

ritposac _ _ _ _ _ _ _ _

Orange foods help keep your eyes and skin healthy!

Andy's Fun Food Fact:

Did you know that if you eat **way** too many orange foods, your skin can turn a bit orange? This is called hypercarotenemia, but don't worry, it's not harmful!

– Andy

Let's Talk:

Together, talk about the healthy orange foods you like. This week, Andy is going to eat these orange foods:

- **Frozen peaches in a smoothie**
- **Baked sweet potato fries sprinkled with savory spices and dipped into hummus or light sour cream**
- **Pre-cut, washed, crinkle-cut carrots with ranch dressing**

 Your Turn: Healthy Orange Foods

1. Choose one new orange food each week to taste.
2. Take small tastes and write down the flavor, the texture, and if you like it.
3. Be a superstar like Andy and include orange foods for a healthy body every day.

 Tip: I Tried It!

When trying a new food in a recipe, pair it with a food or sauce you already like. This will make the new food taste more familiar.

You can also take small tastes. It's okay if you don't like a new food the first time you try it. It can take many tastes to learn to like a food and get used to its texture (how it feels in your mouth). It's like reading, you learn by doing more of it!

"I asked my mom at the store to buy dried persimmons. She said, 'I don't like them,' but then she tried them again and really loved the taste. I said, 'Don't be afraid to try new foods!'"

– Andy

MEET MARCUS

"Hi, I am Marcus. I get my powers from yellow foods. They help me heal things and create heat. I like to garden and help things grow. The rest of the Super Crew rely on me to grow our plants for super fuel!"

Marcus loves to eat yellow foods like:

- lemons
- pineapple
- yellow squash
- corn
- yellow peppers
- golden quinoa

- Asian pear
- dragon fruit
- guavasteen
- golden kiwi
- yellow chilis
- yellow tomatoes

"Yellow foods help keep me from getting sick, so I can play with my friends and think better in school. I love the taste of sliced lemons in my water or squeezed onto my fruits or vegetables. They add super Vitamin C goodness."

— Marcus

Let's Talk:

Together, talk about yummy ways to include healthy yellow foods in meals and snacks. Here are a few to try:

1. Try quinoa and beans in place of rice and beans.

2. Make yellow or green zucchini squash coins. Cut squash into circles, dip into egg batter, and roll in whole-grain breadcrumbs. Add salt and pepper, and then bake.

3. Eat frozen pineapple pieces like a cold snack, or let them thaw in the refrigerator to enjoy later.

Your Turn: Healthy Yellow Foods

Out loud, name which healthy yellow foods you'd like to try! Look up new recipes and see what you find.

1. Choose one yellow food each week to taste.

2. Take small tastes and write down its flavor and texture, and if you like it.

3. Be a superstar like Marcus and include yellow foods for their taste and powerful "fight-o-nutrient" benefits.

Tip: I Tried It!

It takes a lot of courage to try new foods. If you don't like a food prepared one way, try it another way. For example, you may not like cauliflower pieces raw, but like cauliflower cut into tiny pieces and cooked (called riced cauliflower).

Pat yourself on the back when you try a food in a new way!

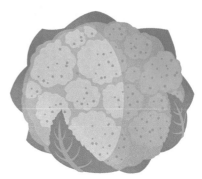

Activity: Marcus' Tasty Food Search

Marcus is looking for a healthy snack. Can you help him find three healthy foods in his refrigerator?

_____

_____

_____

Answer key available at: SuperKidsNutrition.com/Healthy-Eating-Book.

> Yellow foods contain antioxidants that fight off free radicals, the bad guy invaders who want to damage your cells.

> Plant foods have phytonutrients that protect your body from sickness. We call them "fight-o-nutrients."

Marcus' Fun Food Fact:

Corn has an even number of rows on each ear. Next time you're at the grocery store or farmers market, buy one to take home and count the rows!

— Marcus

MEET JESSIE

"Hi, I am Jessie. I get my powers from **green foods**. I can change the form of objects when I eat them. I love science almost as much as I love my little brother Tom-Tom. My friends know that if they need a puzzle solved, I'm the one to ask.

My parents don't need to ask me to eat my **greens. Green foods** are satisfying, make me feel good, and help my whole body!"

Jessie gets her powers from green foods like:

- avocado
- artichoke
- kiwi
- kale
- tomatillo
- Brussels sprouts
- broccoli
- basil
- cilantro

- green grapes
- edamame
- seaweed
- spinach
- lettuce
- limes
- green lentils
- nopales

"I love food science! I think it's so cool how the texture and shape of eggs change when fried or boiled. I love the taste of homemade yogurt from milk. I eat it with golden raisins made from green grapes."

– Jessie

Did you know green foods help your entire body? They're special because they help:

- you see better
- make your nails grow
- protect you from getting sick

I love eating kiwi or grapes in my oatmeal each morning because they give my brain energy to help me do well in school.

"Eat more green foods to stay sharp and healthy like me!"

— Jessie

Activity: Make a Fruit Salad

Circle the fruits below that you want to try. Then write in your favorite fruits that are missing.

Combine them to make your very own crazy colorful fruit salad!

To add kiwi to your fruit salad, cut it in half, then spoon out the insides and toss it in.

Green Grapes + Kiwi + Mango

Strawberries + Pineapple + Watermelon

Raspberries + Banana + Red Grapes

_____ + _____ + _____

_____ + _____ + _____

Jessie's Fun Food Fact:

Kiwi has two times as much Vitamin C as an orange. Vitamin C is good for your immune system to help keep your body healthy. I eat kiwi because it tastes sweet and tart and is so yummy!

— Jessie

Breakfast = Brain Power

BE A SUPER CREW STAR! EAT BREAKFAST EVERY DAY.

Eat a healthy balanced breakfast
to help you think your best.

Jessie,
Super Crew® Kid

MEET PENNY

"Hi, I am Penny. I get my powers from **purple foods**. I can run at super speeds when I eat them. The Super Crew says I'm a natural leader. I point them in the right direction and help them succeed. **Purple foods** are my power fuel. I eat them every day because they're delicious.

Purple foods help your memory and are good for your heart. I like plums, grapes, and berries for their naturally sweet taste. I love the taste of roasted eggplant or cabbage in coleslaw."

Penny gets her powers from purple foods like:

- purple cabbage
- eggplant
- purple cauliflower
- plums
- purple grapes
- mulberries

- purple potatoes
- blackberries
- purple carrots
- figs
- acai berries
- beets

"Eat yummy purple foods to protect your memory and keep your heart strong. Move and play every day to have a healthy brain and heart like me!"

– Penny

Activity: Overnight Oats

Follow these easy steps and try it for your family!

1. Wash and cut up your favorite fruit into a 1-cup serving.
2. Mix 1 cup of whole old-fashioned oats with 2 cups of milk.
3. Add in the fruit, 2 teaspoons of honey, and ½ teaspoon of cinnamon.
4. Mix all ingredients together and place in the refrigerator overnight.

Three ways to enjoy your overnight oats:

1. Eat them cold or warm them up.
2. Top with a little bit of yogurt and chia seeds.
3. Add a couple of tablespoons of chopped nuts for an added crunch.

Did you know that purple foods help:

- keep your heart healthy
- protect you against diseases
- protect your brain cells

Penny's Fun Food Fact:

Purple foods have a "fight-o-nutrient" (phytonutrient) that helps fight off bad things like viruses, bacteria, and disease. The vitamins, minerals, and fiber found in purple foods also help protect your body.

"Purple foods have many different flavors and textures. Some are sweet, and others are savory. Can you think of ideas for meals and snacks that could include a purple food?"

– Penny

I like grapes or raisins in oatmeal or yogurt. When sharing grapes with Super Baby Abigail, I make sure to cut them up, so it's not a choking hazard.

MEET CARLOS

"Hi, I am Carlos! I get my powers from **white foods.** I can create clouds and stink bombs when I eat them. My favorite subject is math, and I love to add and multiply. **White foods** help keep your lungs and blood vessels healthy. They also taste amazing."

Carlos's favorite white foods are:

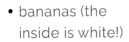

- bananas (the inside is white!)
- white beans
- cauliflower
- garlic
- onions
- yucca
- cassava
- cabbage
- jicama
- potato

"Although I get my powers from white and beige plant-based foods, I also like milk and yogurt. Drink low-fat milk and eat yogurt to build your bones so you can grow up strong and powerful."

– Carlos

Tip: Plant-Based Milk Vitamins and Minerals:

If you drink plant-based milk, ask your parents to read the food label. Make sure you buy one that gives you Vitamin D and calcium for healthy bones.

Activity: Name the Fruits and Vegetables With The Super Crew!

Super Crew kids Marcus, Carlos, and Super Baby Abigail are at the farmer's market. They're buying fruits and veggies to eat at home. With your family, name some of the colorful fruits and vegetables shown in the picture. Then write them in the blanks below. Next, circle the foods you want to try!

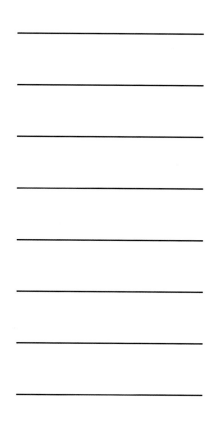

_____

_____

_____

_____

_____

_____

_____

_____

_____

MEET KIRA

"Hi, I am Kira! I get my powers from **brown foods** and herbs and spices. I camouflage (blend in and hide) with nature and float in the air. I love to dance and climb trees. I always carry a few cinnamon sticks in my pocket because they make any food taste better."

Kira gets her powers from brown foods like:

- whole grains
- brown pears
- cinnamon
- brown figs
- toasted pepitas (pumpkin seeds)
- walnuts

- cloves
- almonds
- brown rice
- ground coriander
- nutmeg
- ground flaxseeds

"Add some new tasty brown foods to your diet. I like to try new herbs and spices by sprinkling them on food to see how the taste changes. I love cinnamon's sweetness. It can help fight off germs! Will you try cinnamon with me?"

– Kira

Kira's Fun Food Fact:

Did you notice that the outside of the walnut shell looks like a brain and the inside looks like a heart? Guess what? Walnuts are good for both your brain and your heart! They taste yummy in yogurt, grits, oatmeal, and crushed on top of pancakes or baked fish.

Let's Talk:

Try new whole grains together! Look for oats, barley, brown rice, popcorn, polenta, quinoa, farro, amaranth, buckwheat (like soba noodles), spelt, kamut, or millet at the store! These grains are as rich in taste as their names are funny. Whole grains have many nutrients like vitamins, minerals, and fiber. These are good for growing a healthy body.

> Try making homemade granola or cinnamon rolls with less sugar and use a little extra cinnamon for sweetness instead.

> Your recipes will smell wonderful and taste delicious!

Your Turn: Healthy Brown Foods

Out loud, name which brown foods you'd like to try!

1. Choose one new food each week to have in a snack or meal.

2. Try a new whole grain in one of your favorite whole grain recipes.

3. Be a superstar like Kira and eat brown foods for their taste and powerful "fight-o-nutrient" benefits.

Activity: Build Your Own Whole Grain Meal

Use the handy chart below to make your own delicious meal. Choose something from each step to create a sandwich, wrap, burrito, or bowl. Create your favorite to make with friends and family.

Step 1: Choose a healthy whole grain	Step 2: Choose your veggie or fruit	Step 3: Choose a protein	Step 4: Optional flavor boosters
• Amaranth • Barley • Brown rice • Buckwheat • Corn or whole-grain tortilla • Kamut • Millet • Quinoa • Spelt • Whole-grain bread • Whole-grain flatbread • Whole-grain pasta	• Avocado • Banana • Bell pepper • Berries • Carrots • Cucumber • Frozen, canned, or fresh corn • Jicama • Leafy greens: spinach, kale, arugula, romaine • Sprouts • Tomato sauce	• Beans • Cheese • Chopped boiled eggs • Cottage cheese • Edamame • Fish • Greek yogurt • Lean beef • Lean chicken or turkey • Lentils • Nuts/nut butter • Seeds/seed butter • Tempeh • Tofu	• Cinnamon • Fresh lemon or lime juice • Fresh parsley or herbs, like mint, oregano, and cilantro • Guacamole • Salad dressing • Honey • Hot sauce • Hummus • Mayo • Mustard • Olive oil • Pesto • Salsa • Salt and pepper • Soy sauce • Tzatziki • Vinegar

Activity: Create Colorful Meals Like the Super Crew

Here are meals the Super Crew made this week.

1. Mashed banana and berries, chopped walnuts, and peanut butter on whole-wheat toast

2. A bowl with whole-wheat pasta, canned or frozen corn, black beans, diced tomato, and green peppers with salsa and drizzled olive oil

3. Canned salmon with lettuce, celery, tomato, mayo, and hummus in a wrap

Be a superstar like the Super Crew and make your own yummy meals! Write a few ideas below.

_____

_____

_____

_____

_____

THE SUPER CREW

Activity: I Tried It Bingo!

Directions: Be a superstar like the Super Crew and try new foods. Draw a star around each activity you complete. After achieving a completed row, decide with your parents what your reward for BINGO will be!

Positive reward examples include reading a book together, playing catch, cooking with a parent, seeing a new movie, going to the farmers market or playground, getting a hug, a small toy, or a sticker!

I did an activity in the book.	I tried a new whole grain.	I tried a new purple food.	I tried the same food prepared differently.	I had a healthy breakfast.
I had fruit for dessert.	I tried a new food texture.	★	I tried mixing a new food with a favorite food.	I ate a new food from plants.
I tried blended veggies in my tomato sauce.	I tried a family recipe.	I tried a new spice or herb.	I tried cooking a food in a new way.	I tried adding a fruit or veggie to my water.

JUST FOR PARENTS

Help your children eat healthy like the Super Crew! Here is a list of simple things that you can do to make a big difference in how your children eat. Remember, **how** you feed your children is just as important as **what** you feed them.

Help Children Get the Right Amount of Food

- Respect your child's appetite. Don't insist or applaud a clean plate and don't take away food if they're still feeling hungry. Remember, you decide on the **what, when, and where** to eat. Offer healthy foods, but it is then up to your kids to decide **how much** or even **whether** to eat.

- Teach children how to listen to their body by referring to hunger and fullness cues. For example, ask, "are you full, or are you hungry for more?" instead of "do you want more?"

- Have structured meals and snacks in a designated place. Plan to eat your meals and snacks around the same time each day.

- *Do not allow* grazing on food throughout the day. Instead offer snack time. Kids have small stomachs and usually don't eat enough to stay full from one meal to the next.

- Have them eat off of a plate or from a bowl, not out of a bag or box.

- Teach children to start with small portions. Tell them they can always take more if they are still hungry. For little ones, give them serving spoons that can fit their smaller hands.

- Remember, a child's stomach is about the size of their fist, so don't expect them to eat adult-sized portions.

Times I can provide meals and snacks:

1. Breakfast: _____

2. Snack: _____

3. Lunch: _____

4. Snack: _____

5. Dinner: _____

Healthy snacks that my child likes:

1. _____

2. _____

3. _____

32

Family Style Meal Reminders –
Eat Together When You Can

- Sit together as a family to eat without the TV, screens, or cell phones.

- Family style meals help set the stage! You can put all the food out and let your kids plate their food. For younger kids, a little help from a grown-up may be needed. Provide small, age-appropriate portions using child-sized utensils and dishes.

- Find healthy foods your child likes and make sure they are included at mealtime. You want them to know that you're aware of their food likes and dislikes. Serve fruits and vegetables first or when kids are hungry right before dinner.

- Your child looks up to you! Set a good example by eating healthy foods, and your child will model you. Fill half of your plate with fruits and vegetables. Fill the other half with whole grains and lean proteins. Include low-fat or fat-free dairy, or when needed, fortified plant-based milk that has protein in amounts similar to dairy.

- Say positive things about foods during meals. Talk about other non-food stuff to make meals enjoyable.

- Allow children to eat to their own fullness without pressure to overeat.

Help Children Expand Their Food Choices

- Children are more likely to try a new food if they are the ones who decide to try it. Offer new foods many times and in different ways without pressuring them.

- Try different textures, shapes, sizes, and temperatures. A child may not like chunky tomato sauce, but may love it in a smooth or pureed form.

- Be patient and keep trying. Remember, it can take up to 20 tries before a child will accept, and even like, a new food. Having them simply put the food in their mouth or lick it counts!

- Bring a colorful picture of a rainbow to the farmer's market or grocery store. Then help your child find and name fruits and vegetables that match the colors of the rainbow.

- Cook with your kids. They will be more likely to eat something they helped you make. You'll also be making memories in the kitchen! Give them small tasks like counting or naming ingredients, tearing lettuce, and setting the table. They will feel like such big helpers and be more interested in trying what they make.

- Garden! This is a fun and hands-on way to teach kids where food comes from. It is an inexpensive way to add more fresh fruits, veggies, and herbs to your family's diet. You can grow plants in a pot – you don't need to have a large area. For more information on how to start a family garden, visit SuperKidsNutrition.com, and search garden.

Try These Cooking and Nutrition Tips!

- Whip up a tasty smoothie with fruit, oats, nuts or nut butter, veggies, and low-fat milk or yogurt. Avocado, baby spinach, baby kale and many other whole foods are also good additions.

- Try frozen fruits and veggies for a cool, sweet treat.

- Create your own (healthier!) version of potato chips. Use sweet potatoes, kale, cabbage, beets, or apples to make chips. More color = more nutrients! Cut up your veggies or pull apart the leaves, then coat in a little olive oil (1-2 tablespoons) and bake at 350°F until crispy.

- Play with different sizes, textures, temperatures, and shapes. If your child doesn't like a certain vegetable cooked, try serving it raw. Switch up shapes by cutting food into rounds, strips, or fun figures with cookie cutters.

- Kids love to dip! Serve fruit with plain yogurt 'dip' or veggies with light salad dressing or hummus. Thread the fruits or vegetables onto skewers for even more fun!

- Have a contest to see how many different colored fruits and veggies you can include in one meal. Let your child name and count them all!

- Eat foods that are in season! Seasonal foods are fresher, tastier, more nutritious, and less expensive because they don't have to travel long distances to get to your table. Use the

Super Crew seasonal activity guides from SuperKidsNutrition.com. Or search for "USDA Seasonal Produce Guide" online to find out what foods are in season in your area now.

- Make a placemat from magazine pictures or drawings of your child's favorite fruits and vegetables. Laminate it for a long-lasting reminder to eat more fruits and veggies. Laminating puts a thin plastic covering on normal paper so that you can wipe off food spills.

Avoid Using Food to Control Behavior

- Don't force your child to eat and do not punish them for not eating certain foods. This can create bad feelings. It is normal for kids to be unsure about new foods.

- Do not use sweets as a reward for eating healthy food. This can increase the desire for sweets and may increase the risk of emotional eating. Try these rewards instead:

  — hugs, kisses, thumbs-up, and praise

  — special one-on-one time with mom or dad (or both!)

  — family dance parties to favorite songs

  — their choice of family activity

  — coins for a piggy bank

  — a coupon for something the child wants

  — art supplies

  — special trips to places like the zoo, library, or park

  — coloring, picture, or chapter books

  — play dates

Activity: Non-Food Rewards
I will reward my child with one of these three things:

1. _____

2. _____

3. _____

Create a Healthy Food Environment

- Remind yourself to slow down and don't try to focus on too many behaviors at once. Helping your child form a positive relationship with food develops over time, not overnight.

- Let your child choose between two or three healthy options. For example, apples and cheese, bananas with peanut butter, or carrot sticks and hummus – this helps your child feel independent, but you stay in control.

- Let children help decide what healthy foods to eat. Kids who choose what healthy foods they get to eat are more likely to try them!

- Stock your fridge and cabinets with a variety of nutritious foods. Some foods that are more processed (like chips, pretzels) are fine, just keep them out of sight until you offer them.

- Offer healthy snacks *more often* than typical "snack foods" like chips, pretzels, and cookies.

- Set boundaries and limits. Encourage healthy food choices, and also let them have typical "snack foods," once in a while.

- Try Meatless Monday and boost plant proteins in your family's meals and snacks.

- Eat with your child. They will be more likely to try new healthy foods if they see you eating and enjoying them.

See these helpful resources:

https://www.superkidsnutrition.com/

https://www.superkidsnutrition.com/healthy-eating-book

https://www.superkidsnutrition.com/healthy-kids

https://www.choosemyplate.gov/

https://www.fns.usda.gov/core-nutrition/core-nutrition-messages

Made in the USA
Las Vegas, NV
22 November 2022

60066333R00026